Jesus' Parables of Grace

James W. Moore

JESUS'
Parables of Grace

DIMENSIONS
FOR LIVING
NASHVILLE

JESUS' PARABLES OF GRACE

Copyright © 2004 by Dimensions for Living

This book is printed on recycled, acid-free, elemental-chlorine–free paper.

Library of Congress Cataloging-in-Publication Data

Moore, James W. (James Wendell), 1938-
    Jesus' parables of grace / James W. Moore.
        p. cm.
    ISBN 0-687-03641-0 (alk. paper)
    1. Jesus Christ—Parables.   I. Title.
    BT375.3.M66 2004
    226.8'06—dc22

                                                    2004000729

Scripture quotations, unless otherwise noted, are from the New Revised Standard Version of the Bible, copyright © 1989, by the Division of Christian Education of the National Council of the Churches of Christ in the United States of America. Used by permission. All rights reserved.

Scripture quotations noted KJV are from the King James or Authorized Version of the Bible.

Scripture quotations noted RSV are from the *Revised Standard Version of the Bible,* copyright © 1946, 1952, 1971 by the Division of Christian Education of the National Council of the Churches of Christ in the USA. Used by permission.

04 05 06 07 08 09 10 11 12 13—10 9 8 7 6 5 4 3 2

MANUFACTURED IN THE UNITED STATES OF AMERICA

In memory of
Dr. Lloyd W. Ramer
Dr. Van Bogard Dunn
Dr. Paul T. Lyles
Dr. D. L. Dykes
My mentors in the faith.

CONTENTS

INTRODUCTION

Jesus' Parables of Grace

Why did Jesus use parables, and how do we unravel them and discover their timeless and powerful messages? Let me begin by giving you five key ideas that help unlock the truths found in all of the parables of Jesus.

First, Jesus spoke in parables—short stories that teach a faith lesson—to be understood and remembered, to proclaim the good news, and to make people think.

Second, Jesus saw himself as one who came to serve the needy, and he believed that the kingdom of God existed anywhere kingdom-deeds such as love, mercy, kindness, and compassion were being done.

Third, God's love for us is unconditional; and God wants us to love one another like that—unconditionally.

Fourth, one way to discover the central truth of a parable is to look for the surprise in it. Look for the moment when you lift your eyebrows or the moment when the original hearers of the story probably thought or said in surprise—or maybe even in shock—"Oh my goodness, did you hear that?"

Fifth, it's important to remember that parables are designed to convey one central truth! Parables (as opposed to allegories, in which everything in the story has a symbolic meaning) make one main point.

Parables slip up on us. They flip our values. They turn our world upside down. They surprise us. This is the great thing about the parables of Jesus: They are always relevant and always personal. They speak eloquently to you and me, here and now. In this book, we will examine six of Jesus' thought-provoking parables to see if we can find ourselves and God's truth for us in these magnificent truth-stories. They are, after all, truth-stories for us—truth-stories from the mind of Jesus that can change our lives as they proclaim God's truth for you and me.

1

The Sower, the Seeds, and the Soils: Broadcasting the Seed

Scripture: Mark 4:1-9

One of Jesus' most fascinating parables is found in Mark 4:1-9 (see also Luke 8:4-8; Matthew 13:1-9), the parable of the sower. Or is it the parable of the seeds? Or perhaps the parable of the soils? What is Jesus saying to us through this graphic parable about how we can best serve God and his kingdom? What is the surprising point of the parable of the sower, the seeds, and the soils in Mark 4? What does it tell us is the best thing we can do for God?

Remember the parable with me. The sower went out to sow his seed. Some seed fell on the path and could not grow because the ground was too hard. Some other seed fell on rocky soil, and because the ground was shallow, the plants sprang up quickly but then quickly died away because they had no roots, no depth. Other seed fell among thorns, and there the plants tried to grow, but the thorns choked the life out of them. Still other seed fell on good soil and grew and yielded a great harvest.

Let me point out that the parable accurately reflects the sowing process as it would have been done by a Galilean farmer in New Testament times. Contrary to our modern farming practices, they did it just the other way around. Nowadays we go out and plow the field and then plant the seed; back then, they did just the opposite. That is, they scattered the seed first, they broadcast their seed indiscriminately, and then they came later and plowed the seed under. This, of course, is why the seed in the parable fell on four different kinds of soil. The Path Soil: The hard, "packed-down," "crusted-over" path soil was first.

The second was the Rocky Soil: a thin layer of soil on a thick layer of rock. Because of the layer of rock, the roots could not go down deep, so the plants would spring up quickly and then quickly die out.

Then there was the Thorny Soil.

And finally, the Good Soil.

Now, it's interesting to note that despite the fact that three of the four soils here are very unpromising, nevertheless the parable ends victoriously with a great harvest. That's very interesting, isn't it?

The question is, What is the central point of this parable? Over the years, there have been a lot of discussion, a lot of dialogue, and, as a matter of fact, quite a bit of disagreement about what the main point of this parable is. What I would like to do is outline for you four different interpretations of the parable and let you try to find yourself somewhere between the lines. Let me give you the four different possibilities first so you can move along with me as we develop them.

(1) Some say the point of the parable is with the Soils—that it has to do with *hearing*, namely, hearing God's Word.

(2) Some say the point of the parable is with the Teller—in other words, that it is autobiographical; Jesus is describing his own experience as a teacher.

(3) Some say the point of the parable is with the Harvest—that it has to do with doing your best and trusting God for the future.

(4) Some say the point of the parable is with the Sower—that it encourages us to love unconditionally, to sow the seeds of kindness indiscriminately.

Let's take a look at these, one at a time.

First, Maybe the Point Is with the Soils

Maybe it's about hearing the Word of God and responding to it. This is probably the most traditional and most popular understanding. It can be well documented because the parable, as it is recorded in Mark, begins with Jesus saying, "Listen!" *Listen*, with an exclamation point. And then he ends the parable by saying, "Let anyone with ears to hear listen!"

When you think of it, this interpretation is fascinating because the soils in the story do seem to represent the way people either hear or don't hear! Think about it.

First, the Path Soil hearers would be the closed-minded people, the persons who are hard, crusted over, and will not listen. They hold God at arm's length. They will not let God or God's Word penetrate their lives.

Next, the Rocky Soil hearers represent the persons who are shallow. They hear, they get enthusiastic, they respond quickly, but they fade away quickly because they have no depth, no roots. They shrivel; they wither and die out.

The Thorny Soil hearers would be the persons with mixed-up priorities. They give their time and energy and effort and creativity to all the wrong things.

And finally, the Good Soil represents those hearers who receive the Word of God and work with it to bring forth new life.

Now, there is a danger with regard to this approach: It tempts us to categorize people. That is, when we read the story and we hear about these different kinds of soils and hearers, it's very easy to begin to think that "John" is Path Soil and "Betty" is Rocky Soil and "Bill" is Thorny Soil and, of course, *I* am Good Soil! To do this is to miss the point. If this parable is about hearing, then what the parable is really saying to us is that these soils represent four potentialities that reside in us all of the time.

At any given moment, I can be one of these kinds of hearers—at lunch today, with my coworkers this afternoon, with my child or spouse tonight, in church next Sunday. At any moment I have a choice: I can be closed-minded or I can be shallow or I can have mixed-up priorities or I can be a good hearer. If the parable is about hearing, then the point is, "Be Good Soil! Be a good listener! Hear and respond to the seed of God's Word!"

Look now at a second possible interpretation of the parable.

Second, Maybe the Point Is with the Teller

That is, maybe the point is with Jesus himself.

Some people have suggested that the parable is autobiographical, that Jesus is reflecting here his own personal experience as a teacher and a prophet. Now, if you follow this line of thinking, you can easily see how it would be developed.

The Path Soil would represent the closed-minded Pharisees who will not listen to Jesus' message.

The Rocky Soil—the shallow rocky soil people—would be the multitudes who come out, maybe out of curiosity, maybe just following the crowds, to see Jesus, to hear him, in the hope that he might *wow* them with a miracle. Then they can tell everybody that they saw him, but they don't really understand what he's talking about. They don't understand the cost of discipleship. They are enthusiastic, but they have no depth, no commitment, no staying power, so their enthusiasm fades quickly; it withers and shrivels and dies.

The Thorny Soil might represent the mixed-up disciples. They hear him, but they don't quite understand, and consequently they are giving their energies to the wrong things. Right up to the end, they are thinking of a military kingdom. Right up to the end, they are saying the wrong thing at the wrong time. Right up to the end, they are squabbling over which one of them is greatest and over who will get the best positions in the New Kingdom.

The Good Soil would represent that faithful remnant, the remnant of people who hear the Word and respond in faith and obedience, who accept the cost of discipleship, who pay the price and sacrifice, and who help God bring the harvest. Of course, the message here is to be Good Soil; receive the seed of God's Word, and work with it to bring forth new life.

That brings us to yet a third interpretation.

Maybe the Point Is with the Harvest

Is the parable about hearing? Is the parable autobiographical? Or is it instead about

17

the harvest? Many scholars believe that the real significance of the parable is that despite a bad beginning—three out of four soils are not very promising—despite that discouraging beginning, in the end there is a great harvest.

These scholars who take this position say that this is a Kingdom parable, a contrast parable, a "good news" parable, and that what the parable is really saying to the people is, "Be patient! Don't get discouraged! Keep on trying! Keep plugging away! Stay with it, no matter how unpromising the situation may look, and trust God to bring it out right with a great harvest in the end."

That is indeed the big surprise in this parable: Three of the four soils are bad, and yet, surprise! Surprise! A great harvest results! That is indeed a reassuring point to hold on to, isn't it? Hang in there! Trust God! God is still in charge! The victory will be God's in the end! Don't give up! Don't lose heart! Do your part! Do your best now, and God will bring the harvest in the future!

Well, what do you think? Is the point of the parable about the Soils? In other words, is it about hearing?

Is it about the Teller; is it autobiographical?

Is it about the Harvest; is it about trusting God?

Or, one other thought.

Maybe the Point Is with the Sower, and the Manner in Which the Sower Sows the Seed

Notice this: The sower *broad*casts the seed! He doesn't *narrow*cast it. He *broad*casts it! He sows the seed indiscriminately, unconditionally, generously. He does not judge, he does not analyze. He does not decide, he does not assess; he just sows the seed and leaves the success to God. The implication here is obvious. Our calling is to be faithful! Our task is to be faithful to the best we know and then to trust God to bring whatever success might follow. We just sow the seed indiscriminately, imitating the unconditional love of God.

We are to love unreservedly, unswervingly, unflinchingly, unconditionally! We are to be kind to all people, with no strings attached. We are to be the agents of goodwill and reconciliation. We are to broadcast the seeds of compassion everywhere we go. We are to sow the seeds of loving-kindness on all alike.

Let me show you what I mean. An orphanage

director was going through the mail one morning when something outside the window caught his eye. It was eight-year-old Sally, climbing a tree. She had a piece of paper in her hand. It looked like a note of some kind. *What in the world is she doing now?* thought the director. He watched her closely. He always watched her closely because she was always up to something. Sally was so full of energy that he never knew what she might do or say next. She was a little character with a lot of spunk and a huge imagination.

Sally continued up the tree, and she got onto the big limb that extended out over the sidewalk that passed by the thick stone wall of the orphanage. She climbed out, attached the note to the limb over the sidewalk, turned around, crawled back, came down the tree, smiled broadly, and then happily skipped back inside the building. The curious director walked outside, anxious to see what Sally was up to this time. He reached up, pulled down the note, and looked at the words she had written in printed block letters with her pencil. He read the note out loud. It said: "To whoever finds this, I love you. *Signed*, Sally (eight years old)."

Sally knew how to broadcast the seed. Sally knew how to sow the seeds of love unconditionally. Now, if we knew how to do that, if we took that seriously, if we were to do that intentionally, then we could indeed become that kinder, gentler nation, and we could (with the help of God, by the grace of God) become the leaven in the loaf of a kinder, gentler world.

Well, what do you think? What is the point of the parable? Where does the parable speak most powerfully and meaningfully to you? This is the great thing about the parables of Jesus—they are always relevant and always personal. They speak eloquently to you and me, here and now.

2

The Prodigal Son:
Anxious to Love, Quick to Forgive, Eager to Reconcile

Scripture: Luke 15:11-24

Some years ago, a seasoned veteran missionary in China befriended a talented young Chinese artist. Through their friendship, the young artist was converted and became a Christian. Then the young artist said to the missionary, "I best internalize truth by painting it. Tell me how to paint the Christian faith." The wise old Christian missionary did a brilliant thing. He pulled out his Bible; he turned to Luke 15 and said, "Here, look at this. It's the parable of the prodigal son. Paint this and you will have the essence of the Christian faith."

So the young Chinese artist undertook the project of painting the parable of the prodigal son. His first attempt showed the prodigal son far down the road, trudging humbly, penitently toward home. His head is bowed, his shoulders slumped in defeat. His clothes are dirty and tattered. He is the picture of shame and remorse. Strangely, the young artist depicted the father standing at the front gate like Yul Brynner in *The King and I*. His arms are folded dramatically across his chest. He is looking sternly down the road with this severe "I told you so" expression on his face.

When the artist showed the painting to his older missionary friend, the missionary thought, "Oh my goodness! He has completely missed the point of the story!" The missionary spoke tenderly, and he said to the artist, "Technically, it is a beautiful work of art, but in all honesty, it misses the main message of the parable."

"How so?" asked the artist.

"Well," said the missionary, "the father should not be standing and waiting; he should not be looking sternly at the prodigal with folded arms. He should be running to meet his son! He is overjoyed and relieved to see him alive and well! Rumors had come to the farm that the prodigal son might be dead, and now here he is, alive and well and home. A thousand times the father has looked down that road longing for this moment, praying for this moment, and now here it is. He can't wait to get to his son and forgive him and hug him and welcome him home."

"But many fathers could not do that," said the artist.

"That may be true," said the missionary, "but this parable was told by Jesus to show us what God is like, to show us dramatically God's gracious, unconditional love; to show us that God is always anxious to love, quick to forgive, eager to reconcile."

"I see," replied the artist. He painted another picture and called his Christian friend to come back to see it. In this second attempt, the prodigal looks exactly the same—stooped, bowed, humble, remorseful, and penitent. But this time the artist depicted the father quite differently. Now, the father is running excitedly toward the prodigal son, his robes flapping in the wind, a look of joy and relief on his face. And interestingly, the father's shoes are two different colors; the shoes don't match! He has on a red shoe and a blue shoe.

The missionary complimented the artist on

the painting but then added, "I must ask you about the father's shoes—one is red and one is blue. They don't match. Why?"

The artist answered, "Because of just what you said. The father is so overjoyed to see his son coming home. He is so anxious to welcome him that he grabs the two nearest shoes and puts them on and runs to meet him. It doesn't matter that the shoes don't match; all that matters is that his son was lost and now he is found. He was feared dead, and now he is alive. The father represents our God who is so anxious to get on with the forgiving and the love and the celebration that his shoes don't match!" The father here epitomizes our God who is always anxious to love, quick to forgive, eager to reconcile.

Isn't that a great story? "The God whose shoes don't match"—a perceptive and profound depiction of what the prodigal son parable is all about. But this magnificent parable shows us not only what God is like, but also what God wants us to be like. He wants us to live in that gracious spirit, in the spirit of unmatched shoes. God wants us always to be anxious to love, quick to forgive, eager to reconcile.

When we read the second half of the parable (in Luke 15:25-32), this becomes clear because while the father is gracious and forgiving throughout, we see a different story with the elder brother. He is angry, resentful, critical, and frustrated. The father rushes out to encourage the elder brother to forgive and to come in to the homecoming dinner. But there is no forgiveness here in the elder brother—no compassion here, no celebration here, no unmatched shoes here. Bitterly he turns away, and he misses the party.

The point is clear: God is like that father. God is always anxious to love, quick to forgive, eager to reconcile. And God wants us to live in that spirit. And when we live in that spirit, life is celebrative. When we don't, we become likely prospects for a life of bitterness, misery, and loneliness. Let me be more specific. In the church, in our families, and in our personal relationships, we can live in that spirit. Look at these with me one at a time.

First, in the Church, We Can Live in That Gracious Spirit

I want us to be a church whose shoes don't match—a church always anxious to love, quick to forgive, eager to reconcile, a church always willing to love unconditionally.

One of the finest professors of preaching in America today is Dr. Fred Craddock. In one of his sermons, he talks about his father. When Fred Craddock was growing up in West Tennessee, his father didn't go to church. He would stay at home, complaining about the hypocrites, grumbling and fussing about lunch being late on Sunday. Once in a while the pastor would come and try to talk to him, but he was kind of rough on the minister. "I know about you folks down at the church," he would say. "You aren't really interested in me. All you fellows want is another name on your roll and another pledge for your budget."

Fred Craddock's mother, who loved the church deeply, would be so embarrassed when her husband would talk to the pastor like that, and she would go into the kitchen and cry. Every minister who came would try his best to win over Mr. Craddock, but to no avail. The conversation would always go the same. Sometimes a guest evangelist would come to the church and the pastor would say, "Here's the toughie, see him!" But Fred Craddock's father would say it again: "You don't care about me. All you want is a new name for your roll and a new pledge for your budget!"

One time he didn't say it. He was in the veterans' hospital, dying. Fred Craddock rushed across the country to see his father. His dad was down to seventy-four pounds. Surgeons had taken out his throat in an attempt to save him, but they said it was too late. They put in a tube so he could breathe, but he couldn't speak. As Fred Craddock looked around the room, there were gifts of love everywhere, beautiful cut flowers, potted plants, thoughtful gifts, cards and letters all over the place, and all of them were from people at the church—the men's Bible class, the women's study class, the youth fellowship—every single gift was from persons or groups connected with the church!

Fred Craddock's father saw Fred looking at the gifts. Mr. Craddock took a pencil and wrote on the side of a tissue box a line from *Hamlet:* "In this harsh world draw your breath in pain to tell my story." Fred Craddock looked at what his father had written, and then he asked, "What is your story, Dad?" His father took the pencil again and wrote: "I was wrong!"

Rebuffed time and again, that church did the right thing: They kept on loving. They were quick to be there. They loved graciously and unconditionally. Their shoes didn't match. I want us to be a church like that. I want us to live in that spirit as a church.

Second, in Our Families, We Can Live in That Gracious Spirit

In our families, we need to be anxious to love, quick to forgive, eager to reconcile. Let me show you what happens when we fail to do that. Some years ago, I held a funeral for a young man who had suddenly died in his mid-thirties, leaving his wife and eight-year-old daughter, who was the apple of his eye. The week before Jerry's death, he had given a special birthday present to his daughter—a coin collection that he had kept since he was a boy. It was not worth a lot materially (probably about sixty dollars), but it was a sentimental gift because he had kept it since he was eight years old, and he wanted to pass it on to his daughter on her eighth birthday.

Three days after the funeral, the wife and daughter were visiting with Jerry's mother. The little eight-year-old girl told her grandmother about the coin collection. The grandmother abruptly told them to return the coin collection to her; she wanted it. When they hesitated and explained that Jerry had given the collection to his daughter for her birthday, Jerry's mother told them to get out of her house and if they didn't bring the coin collection back to her soon, she would never speak to them again. Jerry's wife and daughter left crying.

The next day, Jerry's mother came to see me and told me what had happened. Then she asked me what I would do if I were her. I realized that this was an emotional situation for her, so I measured my words: "Now, of course, it's your decision, but if you really want to know what I would do, I'll tell you. You know," I said to her, "you could lose your granddaughter over this, and I don't think it's worth that. So, if I were you, I would go to them immediately and say, 'I'm sorry.' I would say, 'We are all hurting in this awful grief experience, and I haven't been myself since Jerry's death. I was upset yesterday, and I didn't mean those hard things I said. Of course I want my granddaughter to have the coin collection. That's what Jerry would want. I'm so sorry. Please forgive me!' That's what I would do." She looked at me with tough eyes, and sternly she said, "All hell will freeze over before I do that!"

That was twenty years ago. Her granddaughter is twenty-eight years old now. She graduated from high school with honors and did great in college, and now she is happily married and expecting her first baby. Her grandmother has not seen her or spoken to her for over twenty years—because of a coin collection worth sixty dollars.

Isn't that sad? Isn't that pitiful? Isn't that tragic? In our families we need to wear the shoes that don't match. In our families, we need to be anxious to love, quick to forgive, and eager to reconcile.

Third, in Our Personal Relationships, We Can Live in That Gracious Spirit

Some years ago, a minister friend of mine shared with me a true story that makes the point dramatically. It happened in a small town in the South. A young man named William pulled into a service station one Saturday morning. While William was filling up his pickup truck with gasoline, Old Man Johnson came up behind him. Mr. Johnson was drunk. He had been drinking all night, and he was one of those fellows who becomes belligerent when he drinks alcohol. Mr. Johnson decided to pick a fight with young William. Mr. Johnson started cussing at William, challenging him, and hitting him in the back with his fists as William pumped his gas.

Later, William said, "Why didn't I just get in

my truck and drive off? I had been fussed at and cussed at before." But Mr. Johnson kept on and on, and finally, in frustration, William threw his arm back to push Mr. Johnson away. His forearm caught Mr. Johnson squarely in the chest. The older man in his drunken stupor stumbled back, tripped over a curb, and hit his head on a concrete bench as he went down. He was dead when he hit the ground.

Well, as you can imagine, that episode traumatized the whole town. Everybody knew everybody in that little village, and quickly the word spread, and quickly people began to choose up sides. Some said, "It was William's fault! He should have just gotten out of there." And others said, "No, it was Old Man Johnson's fault. You know how he gets when he is drunk!" Tension was crackling in the air, and the town was split into two camps.

My minister friend (who was a preacher in that little town) received a call from William that afternoon. William said, "Reverend, I want to ask you a favor. I've got to go see Mr. Johnson's wife. Will you go with me? She may not talk to me, but I've got to go and tell her I didn't mean to hurt him. Now, Reverend, you may not want to be seen with me, and if you don't, it's okay; I would understand. But I have to go tell her how sorry I am, and I would appreciate it if you would go with me."

The minister and William went to the Johnson farm. By now relatives and friends had gathered in. They were everywhere—in the house, in the yard, on the porch—yet no one spoke to William and the minister. As they walked up, it was like Moses going through the Red Sea—the people parted, and they walked right on through. William knocked on the door. A relative came and said, "What do you want, William?"

"I'd like to speak to Mrs. Johnson, if she'll see me."

"I don't know if she will want to talk to you."

"I know," William said, "but could you please tell her I'm here?"

When they told Mrs. Johnson that William was in the living room, she jumped up out of her rocking chair. She ran as fast as her legs would carry her into the living room. She rushed over to William and took both of his hands in hers. William started to apologize. She interrupted him. "William," she said, "you don't have to say a word. I have known you all of your life. I was with your mother when you were born. In fact, when the doctor delivered you, he turned and put you in my arms. I was the first person to hold you and talk to you and rock you and sing to you. William, I've known you all of your life. I know you are a good person. I know you didn't mean to do it. I know it was an accident." Then Mrs. Johnson pulled William toward her and hugged him tightly. And with that hug, she healed the whole town!

Now, if we could get into a time machine and go back in time to that scene in the living room of that farmhouse in that little town, and if we stood there and watched Mrs. Johnson hugging William, and if we looked down at Mrs. Johnson's feet, you know what I think we would see? A red slipper and a blue slipper— shoes that don't match! Because she was

anxious to love,
quick to forgive,
eager to reconcile!

You know where Mrs. Johnson learned to live in that gracious spirit, don't you? The same place we learn it: from Jesus!

3

The Elder Brother:
The Awful Pain of Feeling Rejected

Scripture: Luke 15:25-32

There is no pain in the world quite like it: the awful pain of feeling rejected. It hurts! It crushes the spirit and breaks the heart. Let me show you what I mean with a true story.

Her name was Veronica. She was a tall, slender, blonde sixteen-year-old girl who looked like someone who might grow up to be a model or a corporate executive. She was attractive, outgoing, personable, radiant, and happy. She was an only child, and her parents were devoted to her and so proud of her. She was a member of a church I was serving some years ago. One

Sunday, she did a youth "speak-out" in our evening worship service. As our family drove home from church that night, we talked about Veronica, about how she was growing into a mature young woman, about her bubbly personality, and about how we were inspired by her thoughtful comments from the pulpit. She was so vibrant, so full of life.

But the next morning, we were jolted awake by the urgent ringing of the telephone. It was Veronica's mother, alarmed, concerned, frightened, telling us that Veronica had been taken to the emergency room during the night and had been admitted into the hospital as a patient. When I got to the hospital and walked into that room, it was a stark, gloomy situation. The drapes were closed; the room was dark; heavy despair was in the air we breathed. There was Veronica—only hours before so happy, so radiant, so full of life, but now, lying there in a hospital bed, weak, pale, listless, almost the picture of death. She was emotionally drained, completely wrung out, so much so that she literally did not have the strength to lift her arms. She could not walk. She could hardly hold up her head.

I talked with her for a moment. We had a brief prayer together, and then as I left the room, her mother came out into the hallway with me. I was anxious to find out what had happened. Her mother said, "After we got home from church last night, Veronica had a phone call. Just as she hung up the receiver, she fainted, and when we revived her, she was physically unable to walk—she was so weak. We called an ambulance and brought her here to the hospital."

"Do you know of anything that might have caused this?" I asked her mother.

Veronica's mother blinked as tears flooded into her eyes. She looked away and said, "Well, yes. That telephone call last night was to notify Veronica that she had been blackballed by the sorority she wanted to join."

Now, here was a young girl, sixteen years old, an only child who for all of her life had had almost everything she wanted. But at that particular moment, what she wanted more than anything was to be accepted into that sorority, and somebody had rejected her. One person for some unknown reason had blackballed her, and the trauma of that blatant rejection was too much for her. She couldn't handle it. She was not faking. The doctors were sure of that. She was just so hurt that it crushed her emotionally, physically, and spiritually.

Here we see dramatically "the awful pain of feeling rejected." Now I want to leave Veronica in the hospital for just a moment. We are going to get her out later, but right now the point is clear: The pain of feeling rejected can be devastating. In fact, feeling rejected (whether justified or not, whether real or imagined) is one of the most devastating, depressing things that can happen to us. I am using the phrase "feeling rejected" purposefully. Underscore the word *feeling*. The word *feeling* is an important one here for a couple of reasons.

First, sometimes we "feel" rejected when we really aren't being rejected—we only *think* we are. Have you heard about the man who had to quit going to football games because every time the team went into a huddle, he thought they were talking about him! Now, he wasn't being rejected, but he thought he was. Let me hurry to say, though, that even when the rejection is imagined, the pain is just as real!

Second, rejection is indeed something we "feel" dramatically; it hurts! Even the strongest persons don't hold up well, or for long, when they come to feel rejected. Those painful feelings can pull the rug out from under all of us. We see it graphically in Jesus' parable of the prodigal son. There we see a depressed elder brother who is emotionally crushed because he feels rejected.

Remember in the parable how the younger brother runs away to the far country, squanders his money in riotous living, but then, ashamed and penitent, he returns home. The father is so overjoyed. He had feared the worst—that his young son might be dead. But here he is alive and well and home, safe and sound. The father is so happy that he calls for a great celebration. But when the elder brother hears of it, he is hurt, jealous, confused, angry. He feels sorry for himself. But more than that, and worse, he feels that the father has rejected him. Of course, we know better. We know that the father has not rejected him at all. In fact, the parable is misnamed. Instead of the parable of the prodigal son, it should be called the parable of the gracious father! Because, you see, the theme of the parable is not the revelry of the prodigal: nor is it the bitterness of the elder brother. No, the theme here is the goodness of the father—the faithfulness of God. The message here is that God cares and that he wants all of his children to be a part of the celebration.

But the elder brother missed it; he mistakenly felt rejected, and it deflated and crushed him and left him spiritually bankrupt. The feeling of rejection can do that to us. It is undoubtedly part of the reason why divorces can sometimes be more wrenching and devastating than the actual death of a mate. Because while death brings feelings of deep loss and aloneness, divorce can create overtones of rejection; of feeling thrown away; of being unneeded, discarded. We are told that this same thing also counts heavily in the trauma of a prison experience, the whole aura of being confined, caged, out of touch, out of sight, cut off, rejected. Similarly, this is why old age is so depressing to some people: Because of our youth-oriented culture, some older folks feel rejected. And sadly, sometimes when tragedy comes, people may feel that God has rejected them.

The awful pain of feeling rejected: It can crush us emotionally, physically, and spiritually. But the Christian faith has good news for those who feel rejected—the good news of healing and wholeness! So when you feel rejected, here are a few simple guidelines to remember.

First of All, Remember That the Feeling Is Temporary, and Go Talk It Out with Somebody

Don't accept that somber mood as permanent! Remember that this, too, will pass.

Fortunately, in some respects, our moods are changeable, like the weather. When my family and I first came to Houston, someone said to me, "Jim, if you don't like the weather here, just wait a minute; it'll change!" And that's one of the first things to do in handling the feeling of rejection—remember that it will pass, it will change. Dark clouds do come, but behind them the sun is still shining. In time, the clouds will pass, and you will be out in the clear again. So remember that the feeling is temporary, and go find somebody with whom to talk it out.

There's an interesting old saying that makes a good point. It goes like this: "What the average patient wants is not a doctor, but an audience." We all need (from time to time) to ventilate our hurts and fears and talk them out with someone we trust. To "talk it out" with someone who cares and to hear back from that sympathetic listener some words of encouragement—what a wonderfully healing process that is!

Second, Remember That the Person Rejecting You Is Really the One Who Has a Problem

Let me show you what I mean. Some weeks ago, I went into a hospital room to visit a little four-year-old girl who had undergone surgery a few days before. As soon as I walked in, she took one look at me and then took her hands and covered her eyes as if to say, "I don't want to see you! I refuse to acknowledge your presence." She was rejecting me because she thought I was a doctor, and she had had enough of them! Her parents and I had a good laugh over her "cold-shoulder" treatment of me.

Now, it was cute in a four-year-old, but I thought to myself that it was a parable for life. Sometimes when people are hurting, they express their pain like that, by rejecting others! So if someone rejects you, it is probably a red flag. That person who is doing the rejecting is the one with the problem, and you probably just walked by at the wrong time.

Third, Remember How to Laugh; Cultivate a Sense of Humor; Don't Take Yourself Too Seriously

I ran across some humorous test answers given by some music students in an unidentified junior high school. When you read these answers, you will understand why that junior high school is to this day unidentified. For example, these students wrote:

"Music sung by two people at the same time is called a *duel*."

"A xylophone is a music instrument used mainly to illustrate the letter X."

"Dirges are songs to be sung at sad, sad, sad occasions like funerals, weddings, and the like."

"*Refrain* means *don't do it*."

"A virtuoso is a musician with real high morals."

"J. S. Bach died from 1750 to the present day."

"Handel was half German, half Italian, and half English—he was rather large."

"A quartet is when four people sing at the same time. A quintet is when five people sing; and a sextet.... I know what that is, but I'd rather not say."

It's wonderful to laugh with children at the delightful things they sometimes say. It's fun to laugh at the comical antics of clowns or the hilarious wit of comedians. But the best humor of all is when we laugh at ourselves! It's a real mark of maturity; it eases our self-pity; it diminishes our pride and saves us from taking ourselves too seriously. The legendary actress Ethel Barrymore said it well: "You grow up the day you have your first real laugh at yourself."

When you feel rejected, remember that the

feeling is temporary, and go talk it out with somebody. Remember that the person rejecting you is really the one with the problem. Remember to laugh and use your sense of humor.

Fourth and Finally, Remember That God Accepts You

God is with you. This, of course, is most important of all; it's the key message of the Gospels. It's the real good news for those who feel rejected! It's the point of the parable, isn't it? The gracious, accepting, caring love of God.

William Barclay put it like this: "So then for me the supreme truth of Christianity is that in Jesus I see God. When I see Jesus feeding the hungry, comforting the sorrowing, befriending [the rejected], . . . I can say: 'This is what God is like.'. . . All through His life, God was saying to us through Jesus, 'I love you like that.' When He healed the sick, and touched the untouchable and loved the unlovable, He was saying, 'I love you like that'. . . when He endured the insults, the injuries, the disloyalties and the cross . . . He was saying, 'There is nothing in the world you can do that will ever stop me from loving you.'"

When you feel rejected, remember that God never rejects you. God accepts you. You are important to him. You are valuable to him.

Earlier in this chapter, we left Veronica in the hospital; it's time to get her out. Let me tell you what happened. After talking with her mother, I went downstairs and made one phone call. I called the president of the youth group at our church, a boy named Ronnie, and told him of the situation. He told me not to worry; he would handle it. That afternoon I went back to the hospital. A minute or so after I had walked into Veronica's room, about twenty of our young people, led by Ronnie, poured into that room. They had flowers, a radio, candy, cards, balloons—all kinds of gifts in their hands and love in their hearts.

They gathered around Veronica's bed. Ronnie stepped forward. A hush fell over the room as he (obviously the spokesman for the group) prepared to say something. He cleared his throat, and then he blurted out some words I'll never forget. He said, "Veronica, God don't never blackball nobody, and neither do we!"

Ronnie's grammar was terrible, but his theology was great. It was just what the doctor ordered. Veronica smiled, and then she began to laugh. Then each young person in that group came, in turn, and hugged her! That day I witnessed a miracle. Veronica was made whole. She went home the next morning. She had been made well by love. She had been healed by acceptance!

This is the gospel, isn't it? God loves us and accepts us, and then he sends us out as healers, as ministers of acceptance, as servants of mercy, as instruments of his love.

4

The Unjust Judge:
What Can We Count On from God?

Scripture: Luke 18:1-7

Recently I received an E-mail message entitled "Things I Really Don't Understand." It had a list of questions for which there seem to be no clear-cut answers. Here are a few of them:

> Why do doctors and lawyers call what they do *practice*?
> Why is *abbreviation* such a long word?
> Why is it that when you're driving and looking for an address, you turn down the volume on your radio?

Why is a boxing "ring" square?
What was the best thing before sliced
  bread?
How do they get the deer to cross the
  highway at those yellow signs?
How did a fool and his money get together
  in the first place?

These questions are lighthearted, humorous reminders that there are indeed a lot of things in this life that we just don't understand.

But let me take it to a deeper and more disturbing level by sharing with you a poignant and heart-wrenching conversation I had some years ago with a teen-aged boy named Tommy.

Tommy came to see me because his older brother, Jake, had just died. Jake was only sixteen years old when I conducted his funeral. Some kind of mysterious infection had invaded his body and quickly and very tragically had taken the life of this popular, enthusiastic, outgoing, fun teenager.

Two days after the funeral, Jake's brother Tommy came to see me, and he said, "I'm a Christian. I really am. I love God, and I trust him, but right now, I'm pretty shaken. Jake was my older brother, the one I looked up to, the one who protected me, the one who paved the way for me, the one I had so much fun with. He was my hero and now he's gone and my heart is broken. I know he is with God in heaven, but I still hurt. I loved him. I needed him. I just don't understand."

Can't you empathize with that boy who was missing his older brother so terribly and who just couldn't understand why his older brother was so suddenly snatched away from him?

There are so many things in this life that we just don't understand, that we just can't comprehend. For example, we don't really understand disease. Why is a youngster perfectly healthy for sixteen years of his life and then just happens to be in a place where he suddenly encounters some germ or bacteria that invades his body and destroys it?

And we don't understand accidents. They are so random and indiscriminate. You start out a day that is like any other day, and then something happens in a matter of seconds, and life is forever different. You can never go back before that accident.

On and on we could go with our list of things we don't really understand.

Why is there so much pain in our world?

Why do good people suffer?

Why do we hurt one another?

Why can't people get along?

And why do some of the best prayers seem to go unanswered?

Now, all of these difficult questions prompt us to raise yet another crucial question: *What can we count on from God?* When we face the troubles of the world, the heartaches of life, the tough challenges of this existence, what can we count on from God?

This parable in Luke 18 points us toward an answer. At first glance, this parable is confusing to a lot of people. It does sound pretty strange when we first hear it. The parable involves two people—an unjust, arrogant judge and a humble but persistent woman. The judge ignores the woman at first but finally grants her justice because she is so persistent. She won't give up, and she won't go away, so eventually the judge gives in and comes through for her.

Now, let me hurry to point out that Jesus was not suggesting that God is like the judge; not that at all! Jesus was pointing out that God is as different from the judge as day is from night. Jesus is not *likening* them; he is contrasting them. This is what I call a "How Much More" parable. In other words, Jesus was saying, *If a selfish, arrogant, unfeeling, unjust judge can help you if you ask, then* how much more *can God, who loves you intensely, help you when you ask.*

I use this "how much more" analogy all of the time. For example, imagine that a woman comes to me and tells me of something bad that she has done. The woman is penitent, remorseful, ashamed, and heartsick over the wrong she has committed. She confesses it in sordid detail, and then she asks me, "How can God still love me after this terrible thing I have done?" I can say to her, "Well, you've told me all about it, and my heart is going out to you. I just want to help you. I don't want to condemn you or fuss at you or criticize you. I just want to help you make a new start with your life. And if *I* feel that way—with all of my sins and frailties, weaknesses and foibles and inadequacies—if *I'm* capable of that kind of love, how much more forgiving is God (who is the Lord of Life and the Lord of Love)?"

That's what we have here—a "How Much More" parable, a "contrast parable." If that unjust judge can help you when you ask, think how much more God can help you.

Luke makes sure that we know what the parable is all about. He introduces it by saying this: "Then Jesus told them a parable about their need to pray always and not to lose heart"

(18:1). This parable means, be patient; don't lose heart; don't give up; keep on trusting; because you can count on God, and God will come through for you.

Now, with all of this as a backdrop for our thinking, let me list three things we can count on from God.

First of All, We Can Count On God to Hear Us When We Pray

When we pray, we are not talking to a brick wall. We are not praying in a vacuum. We are not speaking empty words into the air that hit the ceiling and bounce back. We are not just talking to ourselves. No, we are visiting with God, and God is leaning forward to listen. Prayer is conversation with God. Prayer is dialogue with God. Simply put, prayer is friendship with God.

So, we can talk to God the way we would talk to our best friend. And we can know that God hears us and understands and loves us like our best friend—which, of course, God is.

Last summer, I went back to Memphis for my high school reunion. It was a great experience. I saw people I had not seen in over forty years. I had really looked forward to seeing

Whitey Johnson. Whitey and I were best friends all through high school. We played football, basketball, and baseball together. We drove to school together every day. We ate lunch together most days in the school cafeteria. Whitey was a groomsman in our wedding. We were great friends.

At the reunion, as we visited, I was touched and intrigued and inspired by my conversations with Whitey Johnson. Over and over, he would say things like this: "Jim, do you remember in the fourth quarter of our football game against Bartlett what you said in the huddle on that fourth-and-one play?" And then he would tell me what I had said.

And then he remembered one time in a baseball game against Central High School how he came up to bat with the score tied and the bases loaded, and I called time-out and came over and said something to him, and he remembered what I had said.

It was like that all night long at that reunion. Whitey kept saying to me such things as, "Jim, do you remember when you said this?" "Jim, do you remember when you said that?" "Do you remember what you said the night we graduated?" Suddenly it dawned on me: No wonder Whitey Johnson was my best friend; he listened to me, and he remembered what I said!

I believe with all my heart that God listens to us like that; God hears us like a best friend when we pray. So, we can pour out our hearts to him, and he will listen. He may not always do precisely what we ask him to do; but whatever we need to express, he is ready and willing to hear it with love. He is not like the unjust judge who listens with a tin ear and finally gives in just to get rid of us. No! God listens and hears us with the compassionate ear and the caring heart of a best friend.

Second, We Can Count On God to Be with Us When We Are Hurting

It seems as if it would be easy to feel the presence of God with us in the beautiful, sacred, lovely places of life, or in those situations where we are on top and everything is going our way. But the truth is that God is never nearer to us than when we are hurting. Time after time I have heard people say it: "This is the hardest thing we've ever gone through. Our hearts are broken, but we will be all right because God is with us as never before." One little boy put it like this: "Why are all the vitamins in spinach and not in ice cream, where they belong?" I don't know the answer to that question; we'll have to ask God about that. But vitamins are in spinach, and God is uniquely and especially with us when we are hurting.

I think I know why. Two reasons. First, we are more open to God when we are in pain—more receptive to his help, more aware of our need of him. And second, because God is like a loving parent who wants to be especially close to his children when they are hurting.

A few years ago, I was at the hospital one morning visiting a little girl who was very sick. Her mother had been at her bedside for days and days. The doctor called me out into the hallway and asked me to see if I could get that young mother to go home for a while. He said, "She hasn't slept, hasn't eaten for several days. She has got to be exhausted. See if you can get her to go home to rest a bit."

I went back into the room and said to her, "Tricia, the doctor is worried about you. He thinks you need some rest. Why don't you come and let me take you home for a while?" I'll never forget what happened next. She looked up at me and said only as a mother can: "Jim, you don't really want me to leave my little girl when she is this sick, do you?" Being a parent myself, I understood exactly where she was coming from, and I said, "No, I'll go downstairs and get you a sandwich."

God is like that—a loving parent, not a harsh judge; a loving parent who wants to be especially close to his children when they are hurting.

So, first, we can count on God to hear us when we pray; and second, we can count on God to be with us when we are hurting.

Third and Finally, We Can Count On God to Go with Us Wherever We May Go

Remember how the psalmist put it:

Whither shall I go from thy Spirit?
. . . .
If I ascend to heaven, thou art there!
    If I make my bed in Sheol, thou art there!
If I take the wings of the morning and
    dwell in the uttermost parts of the sea,
even there thy hand shall lead me,
and thy right hand shall hold me.

(Psalm 139 RSV)

The unjust judge wants to get rid of us, but God wants to enfold us in the circle of his love.

Remember how the songwriter put it—"You'll never walk alone." This is the good news of our faith. On page after page of scripture, we find it—God's promise always to be with us, God's promise never to desert us, God's promise that nothing, not even death, can separate us from God's love in Christ Jesus our Lord.

God is with us! That is the good news of the Bible. On page after page of the Bible, that is the great promise of Scripture. We can count on God to go with us wherever we may go.

Our daughter-in-law, Claire (the wife of our son Jeff), was a cheerleader in high school and college, and after college she worked for the Universal Cheerleaders Association, traveling to colleges all over the United States to train college cheerleaders. These days, every now and then, she is asked to go to Walt Disney World in Orlando, Florida, to judge ESPN-sponsored cheerleading contests. A couple of weeks ago, she went to Orlando, and June and I went up to Dallas to help with the grandchildren while their mother was out of town.

Jeff and Claire have two delightful little boys, Dawson, who is three, and Daniel, who is sixteen months. June and I realized once again how smart God was when he decided to let younger people have the babies! We loved visiting with our grandchildren, but we were absolutely exhausted. Daniel, the sixteen-month-old, was everywhere, grinning the whole time. He is so curious and is in perpetual motion. He can open every door and every drawer, even the ones with childproof locks. He loves to push buttons, and he is constantly pushing every button on the dishwasher and on the TV.

Once I had him watching a child's program on TV. I left the room for thirty seconds, and when I came back, he was watching *Bridget Jones's Diary!* I don't know how he did that, but you get the picture. You have to watch him every minute. When he gets into things, he grins and gives you that look that says, "I know I'm not supposed to be doing this, but I'm so cute that I know you're not going to get too upset with me."

Dawson is three years old now, and he loves to shoot basketballs and kick soccer balls, go upstairs to play with his trains, and watch *VeggieTales* videos. After a couple of days of chasing Daniel and carrying Dawson up the stairs, my back began to hurt a little bit, and I thought, *Uh oh! Better take it easy.* In the midst of my backache, Dawson wanted me to carry him upstairs. I said, "Dawson, let me make a deal with you. Let's hold hands and walk up the stairs together. You are such a big boy now. I better not carry you because my back is hurting a little bit." He said, "Okay," and we started up the stairs. Then Dawson looked at me and said, "Gran, do you have a little baby in your tummy?" He had obviously heard that backache story before in a different context.

Well, the answer in my case was no, but at the same time, I thought this: *No, I don't have a little baby in my tummy, but I do have a great God in my heart! A great God who is always with me, a great God who loves me and treasures me, a great God who can always be counted on to hear me when I pray, to be with me when I'm hurting, and to go with me wherever I may go.*

You can have that great God, too! And you can count on him! So, keep on praying, and don't lose heart; do your best and trust God for the rest.

One beautiful spring day, a little girl went for a walk with her grandfather. As they sauntered along, enjoying the beauty of God's creation all around them, they came to a garden.

The little girl ran ahead and found a gorgeous rosebush covered with roses. Some of the roses were still buds and some were in full bloom. The little girl plucked one of the rosebuds and examined it closely. Then with her fingers, she tried to open the rosebud and bring it to full bloom, but it didn't work. The petals fell away and dropped to the ground, and she was left holding nothing but the stem.

Exasperated, she said to her grandfather, "Gramps, I don't get it. When God opens a flower, it looks so beautiful, but when I try to do it, it falls apart."

Her grandfather answered, "God is more patient than we are. He knows that some things just take time and can't be rushed. He slowly and tenderly unfolds the rose, and he does the same thing with our lives. As we grow, we go through certain stages as our lives unfold. We can't rush that process. Every stage is important, so we just take it one day at a time and trust him to unfold the stages and moments of our lives just as we trust him to unfold the rose."

The grandfather was right, wasn't he? Our calling is to live in day-tight compartments, taking it one day at a time, following God's guidance, celebrating his presence with us every step of the way, and trusting God to watch over us and shape us eventually into what he wants us to be.

5
The Good Samaritan:
Eyes Too Busy to See

Scripture: Luke 10:25-37

I want to begin this chapter in an unusual way, with a simulation experience. Look at the sentence below:

FEDERAL FUSES ARE THE
RESULT OF YEARS OF SCIEN-
TIFIC RESEARCH AND STUDY
AND THE EXPERIENCE OF YEARS.

Now, don't worry about what the sentence means. Rather, I want you to do a very simple thing. Just count the number of *f*s in the sentence.

Many people see only two *f*s in the sentence. Most people looking at this sentence see three *f*s, and they feel certain about it. But wait a minute. Some people see four *f*s, and some see five, and still others see more than five. How many do you see?

Let's count them. One, two, three, four, five, six! One in *federal*, one in *fuses*, one in *scientific*; and then there are three instances of the word *of*. That makes one, two, three, four, five, six *f*s. There is no trick to this. There are indeed six *f*s in the sentence.

Now, the question is, what did we learn from what we just did? Several things. Many helpful lessons emerge from this simulation experience.

The main one, I suppose, is that we very often overlook the obvious. Sometimes we don't see what is right there in front of us. Sometimes we miss what is right before our very eyes.

Another lesson is that people with prior experience can help us. I had been through this exercise before, so I knew from past experience that there were six *f*s there. People with prior experience can see things and point out things that those going through an experience for the first time may be unable to see. (Parents love this point!)

Here's another insight: *People* are like those
*f*s. Some leap out at you—you can't miss
them—while others blend into the landscape.
But, here's the point: They are all important! If
you take one *f* out of the sentence, it becomes
distorted, and the sentence is ruined. All of the
*f*s are important.

This simulation also teaches us how important it is to be open-minded, ever open to new
truth, because sometimes when we are
absolutely sure that we are right, we may be
wrong! The first time I saw that sentence, I
was totally convinced that there were only
three *f*s in it. For the life of me, I couldn't see
all of the *f*s. Somebody had to pry my mind
open and say, "Look! Here they are! Count
them!" But up to that point I was certain that
I was right. The point is, we need to be open to
new truth. It's dangerous to be stubbornly
closed-minded.

All of these insights are helpful, but the lesson I want us to zero in on now is this one:
How we look at things is so important! How
we view things is so momentous! Spiritual
vision is so significant! Jesus underscored that
point in one of his most famous stories, a parable that shows us dramatically that there are
three different ways to look at life. He shows

us that we can look at life with cruel eyes or with calculating eyes or with caring eyes.

The story, of course, is the parable of the good Samaritan. I am sure you remember it.

A man is attacked, beaten, robbed, and left seriously injured on the roadside by the robbers, the thieves. They are the ones who see life and other people with selfish, cruel eyes. They say, "We see what you've got, and we want it—and we are big enough to take it away from you!" Some people go through life like that. They are takers, grabbers, robbers. Their attitude is totally selfish. They view everything with this question in mind: *What's in it for me, and how can I cheat you out of it or beat you out of it?* They see everything through cruel eyes.

Then there are other people like the priest and the Levite who see life with calculating eyes. They see the injured man, and they think it's unfortunate what happened to him, but they don't want to get involved, so they nervously slip by on the other side. They don't want to get their hands dirty. They hope someone else will come along soon to address this problem, but not them. They pull back. They see everything with calculating eyes.

Then there is the Samaritan—the "good"

Samaritan. He is good because he sees the problem with caring eyes, and he cares enough to do something about it. He reaches out with love and compassion. He brings healing where there is hurt. He sees everything with caring eyes.

Consider with me this simple outline. These three approaches are possibilities for each one of us. Which one describes you? How do you see? With cruel eyes? With calculating eyes? Or with caring eyes? Let's take a look and see if we can see ourselves somewhere between the lines.

First of All, It Is Possible to See Life and Other People with Cruel Eyes—with Selfish, Arrogant Eyes

That can be your attitude, your basic approach to life. It's an option open to you. You can have a diminishing, destructive effect upon this world by being a cold, ruthless taker who uses and takes advantage of others. I pray that none of us will look at life with cruel, selfish eyes, but the sad fact is that many people do indeed choose this sinful way. They become grabbers, robbers, thieves, parasites. They lurk in the shadows, just waiting to pounce on some innocent persons, to take advantage of other people, to overpower them, and to take away what they have.

Sadly, that's the way some people view life. It's documented on the news every night: murders, rapes, robberies. What in the world gets into people to cause them to do those brutal, vicious, cruel things? Who do they think they are? How can they have no regard and no respect for the lives of others? Where did they get such cruel eyes?

When Jesus was born in Bethlehem, there was a spoiled and selfish king in Judea named Herod. Herod looked at life with cruel eyes. He always negotiated from power. He always looked out for number one. In many ways, Herod was a brilliant man. He was a genius at political scheming and intrigue. He was also ruthless, sadistic, and cruel. In fact, this is hard to believe. But history documents it, that shortly before Herod died, he decreed that on the day of his death, three hundred prominent citizens in his kingdom should be executed!

Now, follow his thinking. He knew that Israel would not grieve his passing. He had been too mean and tyrannical. He knew that they might even dance with joy in the streets over his death. So he tried to come up with a strategic ploy to prevent that, and perhaps even to deceive history as to his own importance and image. His idea was that if he killed off three hundred beloved people on the day he died, there would be a lot of grief in the streets, and history might think that the grief and sorrow were for him. His plan didn't work, of course. Herod died, and the world in which he lived was glad.

People such as Herod, who see life and other people with cruel and selfish eyes, live in every age. I am fascinated sometimes to walk through cemeteries and read the epitaphs. Back in colonial days, our ancestors were sometimes brutally frank in their appraisal of the deceased. For example, in Winslow, Maine, there is a monument to a man named Benjamin Wood, who had been buried in a wooden casket. The words on his tombstone are:

> Here lies one Wood enclosed in wood,
> One Wood within another:
> The outer wood is very good;
> We cannot praise the other.

Sadly, so it is with some people. They live lives that can't be praised. The world is diminished, made poorer by their approach to life.

Let me hurry to say that this selfish approach is not confined to robbers. There are many respectable people who take advantage of others, who think only of themselves, who insist on doing things their way without concern for what happens to other people.

Now, let me ask you. What about you? How is it with you? What influence do you have on the world? Is it constructive or destructive? Do you build up or tear down? Do you give? Or do you take? Do you hurt? Or do you heal? It's something to think about because the sad fact is that some people do look at life with cruel eyes. I hope that won't be true of us, but it is a possibility.

A Second Possibility Is to Look at Life with Calculating Eyes—with Scared, Nervous "I Don't Want to Get Involved" Eyes

In the good Samaritan parable, the priest and the Levite symbolize this attitude. Their approach was, "I'm not going to hurt you. I'm not going to rob you. I'm not going to take advantage of you like those robbers. But the truth is, I just don't want to be bothered with you. I just don't want to get involved in this.

After all, it's none of my business. It's none of my affair. Going out on a limb for others is just too risky." And so they went by on the other side. A lot of people approach life like that— cold, calculating, indifferent, insensitive, always protecting their own best interest.

Some years ago (in March 1964), in a respectable New York residential area, a twenty-eight-year-old woman named Kitty Genovese was attacked, beaten, and stabbed by a man who had followed her home. For some thirty minutes, the man beat and stabbed her as she screamed for help. Finally, she died. Why bring this up now? Because after it was all over, police found thirty-eight people who had heard or watched some part of the brutal murder during that half hour. Not one of them acted to help. Not one of them picked up the phone to call police.

Finally, after the young woman was dead and the killer gone, someone dialed the police. Do you know how long it took the police to get there? Three minutes! Just three minutes after the call was made, police were on the scene. Kitty Genovese might well be alive today if one person out of thirty-eight had had enough compassion to help, enough concern just to call the police. When questioned later, almost every one of the witnesses gave the same excuse: "I just didn't want to get involved."

But Christian love demands that we get involved. Christian love is compassionate, and compassion and action go hand in hand.

It's interesting to note how in the New Testament, every time we read words to the effect of "Jesus was filled with compassion," we should just as well get ready because that means Jesus is about to act, about to do something, about to express his love, about to help somebody, about to get involved. In words and deeds, Jesus shows us how to love, and he shows us how sad it is when people go through life with cruel, selfish eyes or with calculating, indifferent eyes.

Thank God There Is a Third Possibility: We Can Look at Life and at Other People with Caring Eyes

Some years ago, there was a twelve-year-old boy who lived with his family in a small village in Africa. The boy's name was Panya. One day as Panya was baby-sitting his little brother while the other members of the family were at work in the sugarcane fields, their little hut caught fire and was quickly enveloped in flames. Panya was outside, but remembering his little brother, he immediately jumped up and ran into the blazing hut, only to find the baby trapped by a burning rafter that had fallen.

Hurriedly, Panya worked to free his brother. He had trouble getting him loose as the flames danced about his head. Finally, he freed him. He picked him up, carried him outside, and revived him just as the hut caved in.

By this time, the villagers had gathered outside the smoldering remains. They had been too frightened to go inside or do anything to help, and they were tremendously impressed with the courage of young Panya. They congratulated him for his heroic efforts. "Panya, you are very brave! Weren't you frightened? What were you thinking of as you ran into the burning hut?" Panya answered, "I wasn't thinking of anything. I just heard my little brother crying."

How long has it been since you heard your brother or sister crying? How long has it been since you stopped and did something about it?

Some years ago, the great Henry van Dyke gave a classic description of the people in the good Samaritan parable. He pointed out that the robbers came saying, "What's yours is mine and I'll take it!" The priest and Levite passed by on the other side saying, "What's mine is mine and I'll keep it!" The good Samaritan stopped and helped the injured man saying, "What's mine is yours and let's share it!"

The Scriptures describe the good Samaritan this way:

"He had compassion." (Luke 10:33 RSV)
He "went to him." (verse 34 RSV)
He "bound up his wounds." (verse 34 RSV)
He "brought him to an inn." (verse 34 RSV)
He "took care of him." (verse 34 RSV)
He paid for his keep. (verse 35, familiar paraphrase)

Sometimes we get confused about what life really means. Sometimes we can't see it clearly. Sometimes we can't see just what we are supposed to do. But Jesus makes it clear here in Luke 10 that we are to look at life and at other people not with cruel eyes, not with calculating eyes, but with caring eyes!

6

The Least of These:
Do Everything As If You Were
Doing It for Our Lord

Scripture: Matthew 25:31-40

John Powell, in his devotional book *Through Seasons of the Heart* (Allen, Tex.: Thomas More Publishing, 1996), shares a fascinating legend. Read closely, if you will, "The Legend of the King Who Had No Children."

Once upon a time there was a country, whose beloved king had no children and consequently no heir to the throne, no successor. To deal with this problem, the king devised a plan. He sent out his messengers to post signs on the trees in all the towns of his kingdom.

The signs announced that every qualified young person should apply for an interview with the king as a possible successor to the throne. However, all such applicants must have two special qualifications: They must love God, and they must love their fellow human beings.

In one small village, one young man saw the signs and reflected that he did "indeed love God and his fellow human beings," and he wanted to go to the king's castle for an interview. However, there was a problem. The young man was so poor that he had no clothes that would be presentable in the sight of the king. Nor did he have the money to buy provisions he would need to make the journey to the castle. So, he worked and begged and borrowed until at long last he had enough money for the appropriate clothes and the necessary provisions. Finally, he set out for the castle.

He had almost completed his journey—the castle was in sight—when he came upon a poor beggar by the side of the road. The beggar sat there trembling, clad only in rags. The beggar, pleadingly, extended his arms and held out his hands for help. The beggar, in his weak voice, quietly said, "I'm hungry. I'm thirsty. I'm weak. I'm cold. Would you please help me?"

The young man was so moved, so touched with compassion by the need of the poor man, that immediately he stripped off his new clothes, gave them to the beggar, and put on the beggar's rags.

Without a second thought, the young man gave the beggar all of his food and money and all of his provisions. He loved God, and he loved his fellow human beings. Then the young man proceeded somewhat uncertainly to the castle in the rags of the beggar, without any provisions for his journey home. He thought to himself, *This is probably a waste of time now. Now that I am dressed in these rags, they won't pay any attention to me at all. They may not even let me in the castle.*

However, upon his arrival at the castle, an attendant to the king welcomed him warmly and showed him in. After a long wait, the young man was finally admitted to the throne room of the king. Humbly, he bowed before his king. When he looked up into the face of the king, he could not believe his eyes. He was filled with astonishment. "O my king," he said, "you were the beggar by the side of the road!"

"Yes," replied the king, "I was the beggar."

"But you are not really a beggar. You are the

king! Why did you trick me? Why did you do this to me?" the young man asked.

"Because I had to find out if you really do love—if you really do love God and your fellow human beings. I knew that if I came to you as king, you would have been very much impressed by my crown of gold and my regal robes, and you would have tried to impress me. You would have done anything I asked because of my kingly appearance and power. But that way, I would never have known what is really in your heart. So, I came to you as a beggar, with no claims on you except for the love in your heart. And I have found out that you truly do love God and your fellow human beings. You will be my successor! You will inherit my kingdom!"

Isn't that a beautiful legend? And wait a minute! Haven't we heard this story before? I don't know who created the legend originally, but whoever did was surely inspired to write it by Jesus' parable of the last judgment in Matthew 25. Remember how in that classic parable, all of the nations are gathered before the throne of God, and some of the people are given a great blessing:

Come, O blessed of my Father, inherit the
kingdom prepared for you...; for I was hungry
and you gave me food, I was thirsty and
you gave me drink, I was a stranger and you
welcomed me, I was naked and you clothed
me, I was sick and you visited me, I was in
prison and you came to me. (Matthew 25:34-36
RSV)

But look at this. Upon hearing this blessing
from Jesus, the righteous ones are surprised.
This is one of my favorite parts of this story.
Notice that they aren't arrogant or presumptu-
ous or pompous or holier-than-thou. No, the
righteous people are surprised. Not smug; they
are surprised! "But, wait O gracious King...
When? When did we see you hungry and feed
you, and thirsty and give you drink? When did
we see you a stranger and welcome you, and
naked and clothe you? And when did we see
you sick or in prison and visit you?" And the
King gives that magnificent answer that
resounds across the ages: "Truly I tell you, just
as you did it to one of the least of these ... you
did it to me" (verse 40).

This parable shows us that the best way to
love God is to love God's children. This parable
shows us how much it pleases God when we
love and respect one another. This parable

shows us that God wants us to bring the spirit of love and respect to everything we do. Everything we do, we should do it as if we are doing it for God. Let me show you what I mean.

First of All, As Christians, We Bring That Spirit to the Way We Work

As Christians, we approach every task, every job, as if we were doing it for God. Will Willimon tells about a young man who had just finished law school and was anxious to begin his practice. He was invited for an interview with a very prestigious law firm. It was more than this young man could ever have hoped for.

The process was going exceptionally well. The young man was put up in a first-class hotel. He was royally entertained. He really liked the lawyers he had met. They obviously liked him very much.

All was going great until the last moments of the interview, when one of the lawyers casually mentioned that one of their clients was a company that had a shady reputation. The company was known for making lots of money by taking advantage of poor and uneducated people. The young lawyer expressed reservations about representing a company that so blatantly took advantage of innocent people. He was quickly reassured by the other lawyers that everything that company did was perfectly legal. "It may be legal," replied the young lawyer, "but it is not ethical, and it is not right!"

Well, that ended the interview. The young lawyer returned home. A few days later, he learned that the law firm had moved in another direction in their search and had chosen someone else. Will Willimon said his heart really went out to this young man: He had blown his chance to have the job he had always wanted and deserved. "Actually I feel great," said the young lawyer. "I'm grateful that they gave me the opportunity to clarify who I am and what I really want from my law practice. I'm okay. I now have a much better idea of the kind of law I want to practice. I feel sorry for them because I know that many of them feel the same way I feel, but they are trapped in the system and can't get out."

Will Willimon was touched and impressed by the maturity and strong character of that young lawyer, and Will said to him: "What makes you so confident, so bold to live your life in this way?" I love the young lawyer's answer. He said, "I'm a Christian! I'm not just living my life on the basis of what I want, or just by what seems right to me. I'm trying to live my life based on the principles of Christ" (Will Willimon, *Pulpit Resource,* July, August, September 1999).

That young man is on target, isn't he? He's trying to live out the truth of Matthew 25. He's bringing that spirit—"Do everything as if you were doing it for Christ"—right into the work arena.

Sometimes when it comes to work, we forget to do that, and we can get our priorities so mixed up. Over the years I have noticed that there are several different ways in which people approach their work. Someone put it like this: When it comes to work, some recline, some whine, and some shine.

The recliners are those who hate work, and they loaf through it as much as they can. They lie down on the job. The whiners are those who work grudgingly, resenting every minute of it, and who put more energy into the complaining than into the job itself. And then (thank God for them) there are those who shine, those who approach their work and perform their work in a happy, productive, creative way. These people see their work as an opportunity to serve God and to improve the quality of life in this world.

Now, long before Robert Fulghum wrote his best-selling book *All I Really Need to Know I Learned in Kindergarten* (New York: Fawcett Columbine, 1993), Charlie Brown had set forth his summary of life in a "Peanuts" Sunday cartoon strip that appeared in 1975. Charlie Brown's "Good Rules for Living" included the following:

> Keep the ball low.
> Don't leave your crayons in the sun.
> Use dental floss every day.
> Don't spill the shoe polish.
> Always knock before entering.
> Don't let the ants get in the sugar.
> Always get your first serve in.

We like these kinds of lesson statements that concisely summarize truths and meanings about life.

Well, the apostle Paul, in his letter to the Colossians, gives us a great one, the magic key for how the Christian approaches work. He puts it like this: "Whatever your task, put yourselves into it, as done for the Lord" (Colossians 3:23). In other words, Paul is saying, put your whole heart into it, as if you were doing it for Christ. This is our calling as Christians: to bring this spirit of love and respect to everything, including our work. That's the key, that's the priority. We perform our job as if we are working for God. We work as though it's for the Lord.

Second, As Christians, We Can Bring This Spirit to the Way We Speak

We need to learn how to speak to everyone we meet as if that person were Christ himself, in disguise. We need to speak with that kind of love and respect, as if that person we are addressing is none other than our Lord himself, in disguise. When you stop and think about it, isn't it astonishing and sad how harshly some people speak these days? People who supposedly love one another—husbands and wives, parents and children, neighbors and coworkers—sometimes bash one another with hard, hateful words spewed out in a tone that is so hostile and cruel that it sounds profane and obscene.

Some years ago, I was working with a middle-aged couple who were having serious marriage problems. One day the man said to me, "Sure, I talk tough to her, but she can take it.

Everybody knows I was born with a hot temper. I say hard things to her all the time, but she knows how I am; she understands." And I had to tell him, "No, she doesn't! She doesn't understand! Again and again, day after day, week after week, she comes to the church crying, and she keeps saying to me, 'Jim, how can he love me and talk to me like that?'"

Oh, how we need help here! We need to learn how to speak

words of love, not words of hatefulness;
words of encouragement, not words of discouragement;
words that build up, not words that tear down;
words that inspire, not words that deflate.

When it comes to the way we work and to the way we speak, we need to do it as unto the Lord.

Third and Finally, As Christians, We Bring That Spirit to the Way We Treat Others

I have a good friend who is one of the most outgoing, gregarious persons I have ever known. He is so full of life that he can light up a room. Physically, he is a great big guy—a former football player, strong, powerful, and yet he has a "teddy bear" personality. He's a hugger. He just hugs everybody; he is wired that way. He expresses his love with hugs. Some years ago, I heard him speak to a group of young people, and he said something that inspired them and touched me. He said, "When I first became a Christian, I was so frustrated because I wanted to hug God and didn't know how." He said, "I was so thrilled by what God had done for me in Christ. I was so grateful for the way God had turned my life around. I wanted to hug God, but I didn't know how." And then he said this: "Over the years, I have learned that the best way to hug God is to hug his children; the best way to love God is to love his children; the best way to serve God is to serve his children."

He's right, you know. That's what this parable in Matthew 25 is all about. It reminds us that we should do everything as if we are doing it for God. The way we work; the way we speak; and, yes, the way we treat others.

Everything we do, we do as if we were doing it for our Lord. Jesus said, "As you did it to one of the least of these, . . . you did it to me (verse 40).

86

STUDY GUIDE

Suggestions for Leading a Study of *Jesus' Parables of Grace*

John D. Schroeder

This book by James W. Moore examines the timeless and powerful messages found in the parables of Jesus. To assist you in facilitating a discussion group, this study guide was created to help make this experience beneficial for both you and members of your group. Here are some thoughts on how you can help your group:

1. Distribute the book to participants before your first meeting, and request that they come

having read the brief introduction and the first chapter. You may want to limit the size of your group to increase participation.

2. Begin your sessions on time. Your participants will appreciate your promptness. You may wish to begin your first session with introductions and a brief get-acquainted time. Start each session by reading aloud the "Snaphot Summary" of the chapter for the day.

3. Select discussion questions and activities in advance. Note that the first question is a general question designed to get discussion going. The last question is designed to summarize the discussion. Feel free to change the order of the listed questions and to create your own questions. Allow a set amount of time for the questions and activities.

4. Remind your participants that all questions are valid as part of the learning process. Encourage their participation in discussion by saying that there are no wrong answers and that all input will be appreciated. Invite participants to share their thoughts, personal stories, and ideas as their comfort level allows.

5. Some questions may be more difficult than others to answer. If you ask a question and no one responds, begin the discussion by venturing an answer yourself. Then ask for

comments and other answers. Remember that some questions may have multiple answers.

6. Ask the question "Why?" or "Why do you believe that?" to help continue a discussion and give it greater depth.

7. Give everyone a chance to talk. Keep the conversation moving. Occasionally you may want to direct a question to a specific person who has been quiet. "Do you have anything to add?" is a good follow-up question to ask another person. If the topic of conversation gets off track, move ahead by asking the next question in your study guide.

8. Before moving from questions to activities, ask group members if they have any questions that have not been answered. Remember that as a leader, you do not have to know all of the answers. Some answers may come from group members. Other answers may even need a bit of research. Your job is to keep the discussion moving and to encourage participation.

9. Review the activity in advance. Feel free to modify it or to create your own activity. Encourage participants to try the "At home" activity.

10. Following the conclusion of the activity, close with a brief prayer, praying either the printed prayer from the study guide or a prayer of your own. If your group desires, pause for individual prayer petitions.

11. Be grateful and supportive. Thank group members for their ideas and participation.

12. You are not expected to be a "perfect" leader. Just do the best you can by focusing on the participants and the lesson. God will help you lead this group.

13. Enjoy your time together!

Suggestions for Participants

1. What you will receive from this study will be in direct proportion to your involvement. Be an active participant!

2. Please make it a point to attend all sessions and to arrive on time so that you can receive the greatest benefit.

3. Read the chapter and review the study guide questions prior to the meeting. You may want to jot down questions you have from the reading and also answers to some of the study guide questions.

4. Be supportive and appreciative of your group leader as well as the other members of your group. You are on a journey together.

5. Your participation is encouraged. Feel free to share your thoughts about the material being discussed.

6. Pray for your group and your leader.

Chapter 1
The Sower, the Seeds, and the Soils

Snapshot Summary

1. We need to hear and respond to the seed of God's Word.

2. Our calling is to be faithful to God, to love God, and to love others.

3. Do your best, and trust God for the future.

Reflection / Discussion Questions

1. How does this parable speak to you? How is it relevant to your life today?

2. Why do you think the parable has several interpretations? Are all of the interpretations valid? Explain.

3. Discuss what the different soils might represent in the parable.

4. What do the seeds represent?

5. Why would Jesus' audience be able to relate to this story?

6. What causes the Path Soil hearers to miss the message?

7. What things might cause us to miss the message of the parable today?

8. What can we learn from the manner in which the sower sows the seed?

9. How do you think God wants us to respond to the message of this parable?

10. Reflect on and discuss what you think the great harvest represents.

11. Discuss whether you believe this parable is autobiographical—that is, whether it represents Jesus telling the story of his own experiences.

12. Why do you think Jesus begins and ends this parable with the word *listen*?

Activities

As a group: List the lessons the parable of the sower teaches about God and the kingdom of God. Rank the top three lessons by their importance.

At home: Reflect on the condition of your own "soil," your readiness to receive God's Word.

Prayer: *Dear God, thank you for this parable of grace and the lessons it has for us today. Help us to be good soil so that the seed of your Word will flourish in our lives. May we be faithful to you and trust in you so that we may grow strong and live productive lives that are pleasing to you. Amen.*

Chapter 2
The Prodigal Son

Snapshot Summary

In the church, in our families, and in our personal relationships,

1. A gracious spirit helps us to be anxious to love;

2. A gracious spirit helps us to be quick to forgive; and

3. A gracious spirit helps us to be eager to reconcile.

Reflection / Discussion Questions

1. What new insights did you receive from reading this chapter?

2. In what ways is God like the father in this parable?

3. Do you think people are naturally anxious to love others? If so, what motivates this love?

4. Explain what it means to have a gracious

spirit. How does having a gracious spirit change your life and the lives of others?

5. List some of the ways in which your church lives in that gracious spirit.

6. List and reflect on and discuss some small steps that families can take toward acquiring a gracious spirit.

7. List and reflect on and discuss some steps we can take toward acquiring a gracious spirit in our personal relationships.

8. Talk about someone you know who has "shoes that do not match." What is special about this person?

9. Is this parable more about the prodigal son or the father? Explain your answer.

10. What kind of person do you have to be in order to be quick to forgive? What motivates this type of person?

11. Discuss how the prodigal son may have been changed by his experience.

12. How does this parable challenge you personally?

Activities

As a group: Take an in-depth look at the father, the elder brother, and the prodigal son. What are their strengths and weaknesses? Who do you identify with and why? What did the sons learn or need to learn?

At home: Focus on demonstrating a gracious spirit this week.

Prayer: *Dear God, thank you for the lessons of love, forgiveness, and reconciliation found in this parable. Help us to have a gracious spirit and to use the precious time you have given us on this earth to serve you and accomplish your mission of love. May we follow the example of the father in the parable and always be ready to reconcile. In Jesus' name. Amen.*

Chapter 3
The Elder Brother

Snapshot Summary

1. Rejection brings temporary sadness. Remember that it helps to talk it out with someone.

2. Remember that it is the person who rejects who has the problem.

3. Remember that a sense of humor soothes rejection. Don't take yourself too seriously!

4. Remember that God accepts you. You are valuable to God.

Reflection / Discussion Questions

1. Reflect on and discuss how it feels to be rejected. (If helpful, share some examples that illustrate the feeling of being rejected.)

2. What incorrect assumptions did the elder brother make?

3. List any similarities you may notice between you and the elder brother. In what ways can you identify with him?

4. List some of the reasons people reject others.

5. List some typical responses or reactions to rejection.

6. List some creative and constructive ways to cope with rejection.

7. What lessons have you learned from times when you have been rejected?

8. How can all of us be ministers of acceptance? Give some practical ways we can be accepting of others at home, at work or school, and at church.

9. Do you think rejection is tougher for children or adults? Explain your answer.

10. Rejection is a part of life. At times, we all have to say "no" to someone or refuse a request. How can we reject without causing pain?

11. How can both your faith and other Christians help you in times of rejection?

12. What did you learn about rejection from reading this chapter?

Activities

As a group: Use news media to locate examples of rejection and to see the various reactions. Some examples to look for may include court trials, lost elections, people being fired from their jobs, and any situations in which people did not get what they wanted.

At home: Look for specific ways to be an instrument of healing and acceptance this week.

Prayer: *Dear God, thank you for your constant acceptance and love that you pour out upon us each day. We are your children, and we look to you for direction and help in meeting the challenges we face. Help us to be a source of healing to those who are suffering from rejection. May we be representatives of your love in our broken world. Amen.*

Chapter 4
The Unjust Judge

Snapshot Summary

1. We can count on God to hear us when we pray.

2. We can count on God to be with us when we are hurting.

3. We can count on God to go with us wherever we may go.

Reflection / Discussion Questions

1. There are many things we don't understand in life. Reflect on and describe something that happened to you, perhaps recently, that you can't figure out.

2. Discuss the feelings involved when you can't understand or find a reason for something.

3. What are the lessons found in the parable of the unjust judge?

4. How do you know that God hears your prayers?

5. How important is it to be persistent in our requests to God? Why?

6. Reflect on and share a time when God came through for you and answered a prayer.

7. List the qualities and character of God that we count on.

8. What type of listener is God when we pray?

9. Share a time when you were hurting and felt the presence of God.

10. Reflect on and discuss the two reasons the author gives why God is with us when we are hurting.

11. Explain what it means to count on someone. What expectations are there?

12. Why is it important to remember that God is always with us?

Activities

As a group: We count on God for everything. Make a list of all that we trust in God to provide for us. What burdens are lifted because we can count on God?

At home: Reflect on what it means that you can count on God; look for God's presence with you during the coming week. Look also for ways that you can be a person upon whom the people in your life feel they can depend.

Prayer: *Dear God, wherever we go, you are with us. You listen to our prayers and are with us when we are hurting. Help us to follow your example and to be there for others when they need us. Amen.*

Chapter 5
The Good Samaritan

Snapshot Summary

1. There are three different ways to look at life.

2. In word and deed, Jesus shows us how to love.

3. We should look at life and at other people with caring eyes.

Reflection / Discussion Questions

1. What important lessons does the author highlight from the simulation experience found at the beginning of the chapter?

2. How was Jesus' life a model for love in word and deed?

3. In the parable, the Samaritan is the person least likely to offer help, and yet he does. What is the significance of this? What modern-day examples of this have you observed?

4. Explain what it means to have spiritual vision.

5. What do you think motivates some persons to see life and other people with cruel eyes?

6. List some of the common reasons people don't get involved when someone is in trouble. Are any of these reasons valid? Explain.

7. What can happen when we see a problem, but wait for someone else to act?

8. Reflect on and discuss what is important about the way we look at things and see others.

9. What is the link between compassion and action?

10. List and discuss the benefits and risks of being a "good Samaritan."

11. Reflect on and share a time when you were a good Samaritan or someone was a good Samaritan to you.

12. What new insights did you gain from reading this chapter?

Activities

As a group: Divide into three groups: (1) the Robbers, (2) the Priest and the Levite, and (3) the good Samaritans. Offer justifications for your actions on the road.

At home: Look for opportunities this week to be a good Samaritan.

Prayer: *Dear God, thank you for being with us on the roads we walk each day. Thank you for the good Samaritans in this world who are not afraid to act, and who take the time to help those in need; may we follow their examples of love in action. Help us to look at others with caring eyes. Amen.*

Chapter 6
The Least of These

Snapshot Summary

1. The best way to love God is to love God's children.

2. See your work as an opportunity to serve God.

3. We need to speak to others with love and respect.

Reflection / Discussion Questions

1. What new insights did you receive from reading this chapter?

2. Share a time when someone showed you a spirit of love and respect.

3. List some of the reasons we fail to love others.

4. List and reflect on and discuss some simple ways we can show God's love to others.

5. Reflect on and discuss ways you can serve God through your work.

6. How does wealth (yours or theirs) influence how you view others?

7. If you dressed as a person who is homeless, and sat on the sidewalk or in a park in

your city or town, how would you be treated? Explain your answer.

8. When someone treats you with love and respect, how does that make you feel? In treating one another with love and respect, what are the benefits to our community, to our nation, and to our world?

9. What are the traits and characteristics of the "righteous" people of the world as seen in this parable?

10. How has God's love changed your life?

11. List some words or phrases of love and encouragement that people do not say enough.

12. How has your reading of this book helped you? What lessons did you learn about grace?

Activities

As a group: Make a list of people and professions that the world might consider "the least of these."

At home: Reflect on God's love for you, and respond to it in some tangible way this week.

Prayer: *Dear God, thank you for loving us just as we are. Grant that we may love others as you love us. Help us to remember those who may be considered "the least of these," and to respond to them as though we were responding to you. In Jesus' name. Amen.*